Alberta learner's license practice Test handbook 2020

244 driving license written exam questions and study guide.

Wince .N. George

Copyright page

All Rights Reserved. Contents in this book may not be copied in any way or by means without the written consent of the publisher, with the exclusion of brief excerpts in critical reviews and articles.

Wince .N. George© 2020.

Table of Content

Chapter One 4
Introduction 4
Chapter Two 5
Practice Test 1..5
Chapter Three 25
Practice Test 2..25
Chapter Four 44
Practice Test 3..44
Chapter Five 64
Practice Test 4..64
Chapter Six 82
Practice Test 5..82

Chapter One

Introduction

Obtaining an Alberta Class 7 learner license permit is a simple process. Once you are up to 14 years and above, you are qualified to apply for a learner's license permit

This learner's license is only permitted to be used while driving with a non-probationary driver who is more than 18 years of age.

The first information you need to have is that there is no need for anxiety for the exams.

This book provides selected test questions for potential drivers to study and be ready to succeed in the written part of the driving test. With this theoretical knowledge, the practical aspect of the test would be easier to approach.

Questions from this book are extracted right out of the Alberta drivers' manual to help you prepare for the exams to avoid loss of time, energy and money.

Study the material more than once for proper absorption of the content therein.

Good luck

Chapter Two

Practice Test 1

1. **What does a downward pointing arrow instruct drivers to do?**
   A. Drive in that lane
   B. Stop driving in that lane
   C. It time to change lane
   D. You may increase your speed

Answer A

2. **What does this road sign mean?**

   A. No passing
   B. Only trucks are allowed
   C. No parking
   D. No stopping

Answer A

3. **What following distance should you maintain when driving behind another vehicle?**
   A. A following distance of at most 8 seconds

B. A following distance of at least 2 seconds

C. A following distance of at least 6 seconds

D. A following distance of at most 4 seconds

Answer B

4   What does this sign mean?

A. School zone, slow down to 50 km/h

B. School zone ahead, slow down, look out for children and drive with extra caution

C. Loading zone up ahead for school bus

D. Library ahead

Answer B

5   What should you do when a car ahead is making a right turn on the street?

A. Sound the horn and pass

B. Pass on the right

C. Pass on the left

D. Safely pass on the left if the second lane exists

Answer D

6   Unless posted otherwise. What is the maximum allowable speed when entering a playground zone during hours when controls apply?

A. 20km/h
B. 30km/h
C. 10km/h
D. 50km/h

Answer C

7   How do you calculate the total stopping distance of a passing vehicle?

A. The total sum of perception distance, the braking distance of the vehicle, and the reaction distance.
B. The ratio between braking distance and reaction distance
C. The average of braking distance and perception distance
D. The difference between the reaction distance, the perception distance, and the braking distance of the vehicle.

Answer A

8   When you are leaving the highway, you should use ------------- to slow down

A. An express lane
B. Deceleration Lane

C. Acceleration lane

D. A weave zone

Answer B

9 The minimum period required to complete the learners and probationary stages of the GDL program is:

A. 3 years

B. 4 years

C. 5 years

D. 6 years

Answer A

10 What does this sign mean?

A. Hills ahead

B. Dead- end

C. Bump

D. Narrow Road

Answer C

11 What does this road signs mean?

A. Left turn lane control
B. Railway crossing control
C. Right turn lane control
D. Narrow passage

Answer A

12 One of these options about parking is correct

A. You can lawfully park on the bridge
B. You can lawfully park on a sidewalk or boulevard
C. You can lawfully park 5 meters away from a crosswalk
D. You can lawfully park within three meters of a fire hydrant.

Answer C

13 If you see a flagger while driving, you should?

A. Be ready to increase the speed and quickly pass quickly if the need arises.
B. Be ready to slow down and stop
C. Be ready to increase the speed of your vehicle
D. Be ready to take a detour to the left.

Answer B

14 What does this sign mean?

A. Do not stop at any time between the signs
B. Stop only to load passengers
C. Do not come to a complete stop
D. You are allowed to stand in the area between the signs

Answer A

15 What does this sign mean?

A. There is no accessible parking in this area
B. You are not allowed to park here
C. Parking is not allowed except for vehicles with a valid accessible parking permit
D. Accessible parking permit holders must not park their vehicle near the sign

Answer C

16 What does this sign mean?

A. Entrance is prohibited
B. Pedestrians are not allowed
C. Construction ahead, pedestrian is prohibited
D. No crosswalk in the area

Answer B

17 **Refusing to yield to the right of way to pedestrian attract how many demerit points?**

A. 6 points

B. 4 points

C. 3 points

D. 2 points

Answer B

18 **What period does a learner with a class 7 license not permitted to drive a car?**

A. Midnight to 5:00 am

B. 9:00 am to 5:00 pm

C. 5:00 am to 5:00 pm

D. 5:00 pm to midnight

Answer A

19 **When you purchase a vehicle that is registered in Alberta, you must make sure that:**

A. You complete section 131(1) of the registration and duly it is signed by the previous owner

B. You complete section 23 of the registration and it is duly signed by the previous owner

C. You complete section 2 of the registration and it is duly signed by the previous owner

D. You complete section 3 of the registration and it is duly signed by the previous owner.

Answer C

20 What does this sign mean?

A. Hospital zone
B. Playground
C. Pedestrian crossing
D. School zone

Answer C

21 **Following cyclists too closely is not recommended because**

A. They may likely stop anywhere in the lane
B. They always compete with motor vehicles
C. They do not possess brake lights to warn other road users when they are stopping
D. They should be seen as pedestrians on the road

Answer C

22 **What do you understand by the term "skidding"?**

A. When the vehicle vibrates from the top to bottom

B. When the vehicle starts slowing down

C. When the vehicle speed is cannot be controlled

D. When the driver has lost control of the vehicle

Answer D

23 What type of parking is always used in parking lots?

A. Hill parking

B. Angle Parking

C. Parallel parking

D. None of the above

Answer B

24 What should you do when leaving a traffic circle?

A. Signal Right

B. Sound your horn

C. Proceed without signal

D. Signal left

Answer A

25 How does the graduated driver licensing (GDL) program improve road safety?

A. Creating an unsafe environment for all new drivers

B. Creating a controlled, lower - risk environment for all new drivers

C. Creating a complex environment that is full of difficult tasks for all new drivers

D. Providing less support in an uncontrolled environment for all new drivers.

Answer B

26 If you have an alcohol concentration level between 0.05 and 0.85% during a breath test. Which of the following options will you be subject to for your first offence?

A. You will be fined

B. Your vehicle will be hauled

C. Suspension of license or 3 days

D. All of the above

Answer D

27 What does this sign mean?

A. Parking on either side of the sign is not allowed

B. Night parking is prohibited

C. No parking permit is required

D. Parking in the direction of the arrows is allowed

Answer A

28. An allowable alcohol concentration for GDL drivers is:

A. 0.05%

B. 0.00%

C. 0.02%

D. 0.01%

Answer B

29. What action should you take when you get a flat tire while driving?

A. Increase the speed

B. Control the vehicle from weaving from side to side by holding the steering wheel with a firm grip.

C. Apply the brake immediately

D. Your hazard warning light should be off.

Answer B

30. Under the traffic safety act of Alberta, if an injury or death occurs as a result of an impaired offence by a motor vehicle driver, the license will be suspended for how long.

A. 5 years

B. 3 years

C. 2 months

D. 1 year

Answer A

31 **What is the intended use of a parking lane of a highway?**

A. Emergency parking

B. Bicyclists

C. Pedestrians

D. Passing vehicles

Answer A

32 **Your low – beam light should be used when you are within -----from any oncoming vehicle**

A. 200 meters

B. 400 meters

C. 300 meters

D. 500 meters

Answer C

33 **What is the maximum speed limit on a roadways located outside of the urban area:**

A. 80km/h

B. 100km/h

C. 70km/h

D. 90km/h

Answer A

34 Which of the following options about vehicle insurance is true?

A. Public liability insurance policy is for commercial vehicle only
B. Public liability insurance policy is for vehicle worth over $50,000.
C. In Alberta, liability insurance is not mandatory
D. Public liability insurance policy is for all motor vehicles.

Answer D

35 What does this sign mean?

A. Right intersection ahead
B. Stay to the left of the traffic
C. Stay to the right of the traffic
D. The road is winding up

Answer C

36 What does this sign mean?

A. Come to a complete stop

B. Entrance to the road is prohibited

C. There dead end ahead

D. Railway crossing ahead

Answer B

37 What does this sign mean

A. The vehicles shown are not allowed, trucks only

B. Only the specified vehicles are allowed on the lanes during the specified times and days.

C. Avoid driving on the lane on the day and time posted

D. These vehicles shown are not allowed during the specified days and times.

Answer B

38 What does this sign mean?

A. Parking is not permitted in the area between the signs
B. Do not park in this area
C. The area between the signs is for public transit
D. Parking is permitted in the area between the signs.

Answer A

39 What does this sign mean?

A. Driving through the intersection is prohibited

B. You can drive straight through the intersection

C. Turning right or left is prohibited

D. Stopping at the intersection is not allowed

Answer A

40 A train is sounding a signal and approaching within 500 meters, you should:

A. Stop and wait for the train to cross

B. Do not stop

C. Take a detour

D. Accelerate fast and cross the track

Answer A

41 What should you do when turning right from a two- way road into another?

A. Stay focus in your turning lane

B. Turn to the left lane

C. Swing wide to the left before turning

D. All of the above

Answer A

42 A person with class 6 operator's license may operate which of the vehicles in the option?

A. An ambulance

B. A bus

C. A motorcycle

D. A heavy goods truck

Answer C

43 What does this sign mean?

A. Construction zone ahead
B. Traffic lights ahead
C. Drive slowly
D. Detour ahead

Answer B

44 When a vehicle is passing you on a two-lane highway. What should you do?

A. Stop immediately
B. Move slowly to your right side of the lane
C. Move slightly to your right side of the lane
D. Move quickly to your left side of the lane.

Answer C

45 When the head restraints is well positioned, it can greatly reduce:

A. The driving speed of the vehicles
B. The danger of whiplash injuries in rear-end collisions
C. The collisions that happen in railway crossing
D. The temperature of the body while driving

Answer B

46 Unless posted otherwise, the speed limit for both urban and rural school zones is:

A. 20 km/h
B. 30km/h
C. 40km/h
D. 50km/h

Answer B

47 Route marker sign on the road are used to:

A. Display the combination of roads
B. Indicates names, numbers or designations of roads
C. Indicates the availability of road service
D. Indicate the distance to a destination

Answer B

48 A red "X" above your lane means:

A. Change lanes
B. Slow down for pedestrians
C. Maintain your lane
D. Look out for hazard

Answer A

49 In which situation are U-turns permitted in urban areas?

A. At an alley intersection

B. At a traffic control signal intersection

C. Where there is a sign showing that U-turns are permitted

D. In a roadway in between an intersection

Answer C

50 Which lane should a slower vehicle use when driving on multi- lane highways?

A. The left lane

B. The far right lane

C. The middle lane

D. Any lane

Answer B

Chapter Three

Practice Test 2

1. **Under ideal condition, the maximum speed limit for a school bus (with or without passenger) is:**
   A. 80km/h
   B. 90km/h
   C. 65km/h
   D. 120km/h

Answer B

2. **Road test failures are an outcome from:**
   A. Lack of skill/ control
   B. Unsafe acts
   C. Difficulty adhering to traffic laws
   D. All of the above

Answer D

3. **Indicating your plan before turning or changing lanes:**
   A. It is good only when other road users are in the vicinity
   B. It is required by the highway safety code
   C. It is only needed when you are taking a driving test
   D. It is only required if there is a car behind you.

Answer B

4. **When is it permitted to do a U-turn outside urban areas?**
A. On a curve
B. Never
C. During day time
D. When it can be done safely without interfering with other road users.

Answer D

5. **When you are approaching an intersection with steady amber light, you must:**
A. Proceed through without stopping
B. Come to a complete stop before proceeding
C. Yield to the other vehicles on the right
D. Proceed with the same speed

Answer B

6. **You must adhere to the following options before passing another vehicle on a two - lane road except:**
A. Exceeding the speed limit when passing another vehicle
B. Check the mirrors
C. Check if the road ahead is clear before attempting to pass

D. Turn on your left signal

Answer A

7. **What should you do on a city street when the car ahead is making a right turn?**
A. Pass on the left side
B. Pass on the right side
C. Pass on the left side if there is a second lane, and you can safely do it.
D. Sound your horn continuously as you are about to pass.

Answer C

8. **What should you do if you felt tired while driving?**
A. Stop for a short nap and walk around your vehicle
B. Listen to loud music
C. Drive slowly
D. Let the windows open for fresh air

Answer A

9. **What is the time frame required by the law to notify Alberta Registries of a name and address change:**
A. Within 7 days
B. Within 3 months

C. Immediately

D. Within 14 days

Answer C

10. **If you have a front flat tire, your vehicle will pull strongly towards:**

A. The side of the road

B. The side that has the flat tire

C. The left side

D. The right side

Answer B

11. **What is the significance of white lines on the road?**

A. It separate traffic going in the same direction

B. It separate traffic going in the opposite direction

C. It shows construction zones

D. It shows that lane changing is permitted

Answer A

12. **In the province of Alberta, the license plate stays with the:**

A. Vehicle owner

B. Insurance company

C. Office of the registry

D. Vehicle

Answer A

13. What does a white "X" in a lane mean?

A. It is a reserved lane for parking

B. You are close to a railway crossing

C. The lane is for buses

D. Pedestrians lane, do not trespass

Answer B

14. What does this sign mean?

A. Railway crossing this way

B. Traffic may go in one direction only

C. Exit way

D. Keep to the right of the island

Answer B

15. What does this sign mean?

A. You are heading towards a school zone crossway

B. You are in a school zone
C. All vehicles must stop at the sides of the road where the school bus is
D. All vehicles must stop completely for a school bus in all direction when lights are flashing

Answer D

16. What does this sign mean?

A. The vehicle in lanes 1, 2 or 3 must travel in the direction of their arrows
B. The driver in lane 3 must go straight before turning right
C. The vehicle in lane 1 must go straight before turning left
D. Driver in lane 2 is free o go in any direction

Answer A

17. What does this sign mean?

A. Left turns is not allowed during the posted days
B. A left turn is not allowed at the intersection
C. No left turn allowed during the rush hours
D. U-turn is not allowed during the posted times

Answer A

18. What does this sign mean?

A. Left turns is not allowed
B. You may drive in the opposite direction
C. U - turns are not allowed
D. Turning left at the intersection is not allowed

Answer C

19. What does this sign means

A. Stop for pedestrians to cross
B. Proceed you have the right of way
C. You must allow the traffic in the intersection or close to it to go first
D. Construction zone ahead, drive with caution

Answer C

20. What does this sign means

A. The speed limit is 50km/h ahead
B. The speed limit is 50km/h
C. The speed limit is 50km/h till the next speed sign
D. The speed limit is 50km/h for a distance of 50km/h

Answer A

21. What does this sign mean?

A. You are allowed to turn right only on a red light
B. No right turn is allowed
C. No entering on a red light
D. No turning right on a red light

Answer D

22. Which of the following statements is true for child restraints according to motor vehicle law in Alberta

A. Any child who is below 6 years of age and whose weight is not more than 18 kgs must be correctly restrained in a child safety seat.
B. Any child who is below 9 years of age and whose weight is not more than 25 kgs must be correctly restrained in a child safety seat.
C. Any child who is below 8 years of age and whose weight is not more 20 kgs must be correctly restrained in a child safety seat
D. Any child who is below 7 years of age and whose weight is not more 19 kgs must be correctly restrained in a child safety seat

Answer A

23. **Spots behind or beside your vehicle when you find it difficult to see other vehicles or pedestrians are known as**
    A. Zero spots
    B. Blind Spots
    C. No spots
    D. Invisible Spots

Answer B

24. **A 75 - year - old an above that applies for an operator's license or needs to renew a license must do one of the following options.**
    A. Submit proof of age document
    B. File a medical report and undergo a vision screening
    C. Submit a marriage certificate
    D. An earnings report must be filed

Answer B

25. **What must cyclists and their passengers under 18 years of age wear according to Alberta Road safety law?**
    A. Permitted bicycle safety helmet
    B. Permitted goggles
    C. Permitted safety belt
    D. Permitted uniform

Answer A

26. What should a driver that is involved in an accident do when the overall damage exceeds $2,000?

   A. Call the police and leave the scene immediately
   B. Call the police and stay in the scene
   C. Refuse to report the accident to the police
   D. Clear the accident scene with other drivers

Answer B

27. Drivers of single motor farm vehicles registered in Alberta must have an exception of:

   A. Zero blood alcohol level
   B. Fully licensed instructor
   C. An air brake endorsement
   D. Proof of age certificate

Answer C

28. When trying to use the second exit at the traffic circle, it is advisable to use:

   A. The left - hand lane
   B. The right - hand lane
   C. The middle of the lane
   D. A marked roadway

Answer A

29. Flashing yellow lights indicates:
A. Move faster than normal
B. Proceed with caution
C. No yielding
D. Come to a complete stop

Answer B

30. A vehicle that has flashing amber and red lights indicate:
A. A snowplow vehicle ahead
B. A construction vehicle ahead
C. A goods vehicle ahead
D. A long haul truck ahead

Answer A

31. The places where the highway entrance and exit use the same lane are called:
A. Safety zones
B. Restricted zones
C. Weave Zones
D. Hill zones

Answer C

32. A driver should avoid one of the options below while emerging and approaching the end of the acceleration lane

A. Signal
B. Look in the mirror
C. Slow down or stop the vehicle
D. Increase the speed

Answer C

33. A fully licensed driver if within 2 years has accumulated 15 or more demerit points will:

A. Lose the vehicle
B. Lose the license for some time
C. Go to jail
D. Lose the license indefinitely

Answer B

34. A driver who has suspended licenses and also a code 2 on their notice of suspension must attend one of the following programs.

A. A Screening program for vision
B. Suspension program
C. Impaired driving program (impact)
D. Impaired driving program (planning**)**

Answer C

35. The work of an ABS device in vehicles is to assist drivers in performing:

A. Repair of a flat tire

B. An emergency right turn

C. An emergency left turn

D. An emergency stop

Answer D

36. What do white or bright lights at the rear of a vehicle mean?

A. Stopping vehicle

B. Parked vehicle

C. The vehicle is in reverse

D. Turning vehicle

Answer C

37. What should be the distance between your head and the head restraint to be able to reduce whiplash injuries?

A. More than 15cm (>5.9 inches)

B. Less than 10 cm (< 4 inches)

C. Less than 1 cm (<0.4 inches)

D. More than 10 cm (> 4 inches)

Answer B

38. The safest stopping distance from the nearest rail at a stop sign near a railway crossing is:

A. No closer than 7 meters and not more than 16 meters

B. No closer than 5 meters and not more than 15 meters
   C. No closer than 6 meters and not more than 18 meters
   D. No closer than 8 meters and not more than 20 meters

Answer B

39. **Before the intersection, drivers should be in the proper turning lane at least**
    A. 10 meters
    B. 20 meters
    C. 15 meters
    D. 25 meters

Answer C

40. **On what condition can you drive side by side with a motorcycle in one lane?**
    A. When you are driving a small car
    B. Whenever possible
    C. Never
    D. In heavy traffic only

Answer C

41. **What light should you use when driving in heavy fog**

A. Low beam lights
B. No lights
C. Hazard lights
D. High beam lights

Answer A

42. **Drivers licensed under the graduated driver license program are limited from operating a vehicle**

A. During daytime
B. With alcohol blood level of over .08
C. Without a supervisor
D. When any quantity of alcohol has been consumed

Answer B

43. **If a driver has a prior alcohol offence in the last 10 years, and of recent was found guilty of driving with a blood alcohol concentration over 0.8. Such a driver is disqualified from holding an operator's license for:**

A. 9 months from the onset of conviction
B. 12 months from onset of conviction
C. 36 months from the onset of conviction
D. 6 months from the onset of conviction

Answer C

44. Yellow mark at the center of the road means:

A. That lane changing is permitted
B. Construction zones
C. To separate traffic traveling in the opposite direction
D. To separate traffic traveling in the same direction

Answer C

45. Which direction will you steer when trying to recover from skid?

A. Steer straight ahead
B. Steer the vehicle in the direction you would like it to go
C. Steer in the opposite direction of the road
D. Brake hard to stop the skid

Answer B

46. When you are involved in an accident and fail to remain in the scene of the accident. You will be recorded with what number of demerit points against your license?

A. 4 points
B. 5 points
C. 7 points
D. 12 points

Answer C

47. **What does a broken yellow line in the center of a lane indicate:**
    A. Passing is not allowed
    B. Lane changing is not allowed
    C. Passing permitted only in one direction
    D. There is enough sight distance available to allow passing.

Answer D

48. **Unless stated otherwise. When you want to enter the main street from the alley, road, driveway, or parking lot, what must you do?**
    A. Stop before you enter
    B. Signal with your hand, and then proceed
    C. Look out for pedestrians and vehicles
    D. Proceed with caution while sounding your horn

Answer A

49. **Inability to yield right of way to pedestrians attract how many demerit points against your license.**
    A. 5 points
    B. 4 points
    C. 3 points
    D. 6 points

Answer B

50. Failure to stop for school bus attracts how many demerit points recorded against your license.

A. 5 points
B. 4 points
C. 3 points
D. 6 points

Answer D

Chapter Four

Practice Test 3

1. When a pedestrian is facing a flashing or steady hand or do not walk sign, what should the pedestrian do?
   A. Cross slowly
   B. Ignore and continue
   C. Take a chance and cross
   D. Do not cross the street

Answer D

2. What does this sign mean?

   A. Narrow road ahead
   B. No turning right or left
   C. Railway crossing ahead
   D. The lane is branching off ahead

Answer D

3. **What distance should you give while following a log hauling truck?**

A. 15m

B. 5m

C. 9m

D. 7m

Answer C

4. **What does it mean when you press down on the clutch in a vehicle that has a manual transmission?**

A. It disconnects the engine and the transmission

B. It connects the engine and the transmission

C. It maximizes engine revolutions

D. It decreases engine revolutions

Answer A

5. **What action will you take when another vehicle is merging into your lane from the right?**

A. Stick out your hand to warn the other vehicle to yield

B. Slow down your vehicle and let it merge

C. Ignore and speed up

D. None of the above

Answer C

6. **A 4way intersection has stop signs on all corners, and two vehicles arrive at the intersection at the same time. Which of the vehicle has the right of way?**

A. The vehicle with the longest length
B. The vehicle with the highest speed
C. The vehicle approaching from the right
D. The vehicle approaching from the left

Answer C

7. **What is the time frame persons moving to Alberta must exchange their previous license for an Alberta driver's license?**

A. 60 days
B. 90 days
C. 30 days
D. 120 days

Answer B

8. **You must report to the police or local law enforcement if you are involved in a collision and the overall damage exceeds**

A. $2000
B. $100
C. $500
D. $50

Answer A

9. **In which direction should you turn your front wheels when you are parking facing uphill on the street without a curb?**

    A. Straight ahead
    B. To the left close to the middle of the road
    C. To the right towards the edge of the road
    D. All of the above

Answer C

10. **From the beginning of the graduated driver licensing program, what is the least number of years it will take to exit the program?**

    A. 2
    B. 3
    C. 1
    D. 4

Answer B

11. **What should you do when an emergency vehicle sounding its siren is approaching from behind on a one - way street?**

    A. Pullover to the curb on the left
    B. Pullover to the closest curb
    C. Pullover to the curb on the right
    D. Speed up till you get to the end of the street

Answer B

12. **Where should you begin your turn when you want to turn from one two way road into another?**

A. Anywhere you like

B. Very far to the left

C. Towards the right - hand edge or curb

D. At the middle of the road

Answer C

13. **What should you do if your vehicle is hydroplaning?**

A. Lightly apply the brake

B. Accelerate fast

C. Stay off the brake and accelerator

D. Press hard on the brake

Answer C

14. **When do you give funeral processions right of way**

A. At all times

B. If the speed limit is over 50km/h

C. At rush hour

D. If the light is against them

Answer A

15. What does this sign mean?

   A. A pedestrian crosswalk
   B. A playground
   C. A school zone
   D. Blind people only

Answer C

16. What must you "see" when you are driving behind a large commercial vehicle.
   A. The vehicle registration plate
   B. The side mirrors
   C. The vehicle right - hand side mirror
   D. The vehicle left - hand side mirror

Answer B

17. A child below 6 years of age and not more than--------kg must be restrained in a car with an approved child safety seat.
   A. 22kg
   B. 12kg
   C. 15kg

D. 18kg

Answer D

18. What is the distance you must stop within the intersecting roadway when you are heading towards a stop sign at an intersection with no marked crosswalk or stop line?
    A. 3m
    B. 4m
    C. 2m
    D. 5m

Answer A

19. What action should you take when you notice that your vehicle is having mechanical problems?
    A. Stop anywhere to make a repair
    B. Change lanes safely and move off the road to make a repair
    C. Allow all the passengers to remain in the vehicle
    D. Try to repair it there on the roadside

Answer B

20. What object is the driver of a motor vehicle not permitted to carry "in a house" or "boat trailer?"
    A. Pets

B. Firearms

C. Flammable material

D. Persons

Answer D

21. What should you do at an uncontrolled intersection?

A. Yield right of way to the vehicle on your right

B. Yield right of way to the vehicle on the left

C. Yield right of way to the oncoming vehicle

D. Yield right of way to a fast - moving vehicle

Answer A

22. The hand and arm signal for slowing or stopping a vehicle are:

A. Arm out and pointing down

B. Arm out and pointing up

C. A circular motion

D. Arm straight out of the window

Answer A

23. What distance should you give when parking near a fire hydrant?

A. 5m
B. 2m
C. 1m
D. 4m

Answer A

24. Unless stated otherwise, what is the maximum speed limit on a provincial highway outside an urban area?

A. 90km/h
B. 100km/h
C. 60km/h
D. 50kn/h

Answer B

25. What should you do if there is tire blow out?

A. Allow your foot to stay on the brake and steer to the right
B. Press the brake pedal hard
C. Take your foot off from the gas pedal and move the vehicle firmly in your destination
D. With your foot still on the brake, steer to the left

Answer C

26. A pedestrian using a white cane shows that:

A. The pedestrian is free to walk on a road

B. The pedestrian is deaf

C. The pedestrian wants assistance

D. The pedestrian is blind

Answer D

27. Always drive at a speed that will permit you to:

A. Stop within 90m

B. Stop with a safe distance

C. Stop with 60 m

D. Stop within 150m

Answer B

28. Police officer controlling the traffic overrules:

A. All the traffic signals and signs

B. Traffic signals, but no traffic signs

C. Traffic signs, but no traffic signals

D. None of the above

Answer A

29. What is the advantage of wearing a seat belt in a collision?

A. Make no difference

B. Maximize chances of being injured or killed

C. Minimize chances of being injured or killed

D. Make recovering from vehicle hard

Answer C

30. Moving at high speed increases fuel consumption. How much fuel will you burn for every 10km/h above 90km/h?

A. 10%
B. 15%
C. 5%
D. 25%

Answer A

31. What does this sign mean?

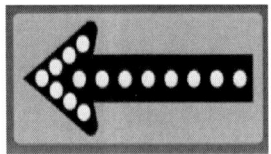

A. Flashing lights on the arrows show the way to follow
B. The Construction zone starts in the direction of the arrow.
C. Traffic must travel in one way only
D. Lane exit ahead

Answer A

32. What does this sign mean?

A. Airport route
B. The landing area for airplane
C. Air show ahead
D. Parking area for airplane

Answer A

33. What does this sign mean?

A. Construction work is 1km ahead
B. Fallen rock ahead
C. Road closure ahead
D. Survey crew assessing road ahead

Answer A

34. What does this sign mean:

A. Stop at the intersection
B. Stop sign ahead
C. Slow down and be prepared to stop
D. Slow down. Stop and leave the construction site

Answer C

35. What does this sign mean?

A. Wheelchair crossing ahead
B. Vehicles that shows accessible parking permit only
C. It shows facilities that are accessible by wheelchair
D. Hospital ahead

Answer C

36. What does this sign mean?

A. Change lane in the arrow direction.
B. Intersection ahead
C. This lane must turn left
D. Lane closed; adjust speed to merge with traffic in lane specified by the arrow

Answer D

37. What does this sign mean?

A. Traffic controller ahead
B. Construction flagger ahead
C. Road work ahead
D. Surveyors ahead

Answer C

38. What does this sign mean?

A. Show lanes direction
B. Shows town and cities distance
C. Shows ways to nearby town and cities
D. Show cities or towns provincial parks post

Answer C

39. What does this sign mean?

A. Shows direction to the passenger railway station
B. Railway crossing ahead
C. Train parking ahead
D. Train workshop ahead

Answer A

40. What does this sign mean?

A. Roadwork going on

B. Construction zone

C. Survey crew ahead

D. Traffic control ahead

Answer D

41. What distance should you get to before you switch to low beam headlights when approaching an oncoming vehicle at night?

A. 300m

B. 200m

C. 150m

D. 100m

Answer A

A. Even with the posted speed limit, when passing a tow truck or emergency vehicles that are stopped with flashing light - activated, what speed must you not exceed?

B. 50km/h

C. 55km/h

D. 70km/h

E. 60km/h

Answer D

42. **What should you do when you enter a curve, and your vehicle begins to skid due to wet conditions?**

A. Take your foot off from the accelerator and brake, just steer.

B. Press hard on the brake

C. Pull - on the parking brake

D. Accelerate the vehicle out of the skid

Answer A

43. **How many seconds will you be scanning ahead while driving in an urban area**

A. 2-5 seconds

B. 7-10 seconds

C. 5-8 seconds

D. 12-15 seconds

Answer D

44. **What is the difference between a traffic circle and a roundabout?**

A. The midpoint island of a roundabout is smaller than the midpoint island of a traffic circle.

B. Pedestrian crossings on roundabouts are located in the center of the intersection for safety.
C. The midpoint island of traffic is smaller than the midpoint island of a roundabout
D. A traffic circle has a close-fitting curve around the island

Answer A

45. What is the maximum speed to slow down when you see a sign that has flashing yellow lights on it?
A. 50km/h
B. 30km/h
C. 40km/h
D. 10km/h

Answer B

46. What is the access distance you must give when you want to park your vehicle near the garage, private roadway, or driveway?
A. 1.5m
B. 2m
C. 2.5m
D. 0.5m

Answer A

47. In case if you want to make a u - turn outside an urban area, make sure other drivers can see you. What are the distances in both directions?

A. 100m
B. 150m
C. 200m
D. 50m

Answer B

48. What does this sign mean?

A. Turning left is not permitted
B. Roads split ahead
C. There is an exit of two right lanes to Brampton Street
D. A sign to assist the drivers in choosing the right lane exit to Brampton Street

Answer D

49. What does this sign mean?
A. Exits only on the right lane
B. The left lane is not allowed after the exit

C. Highway exit ahead

D. None of the above

Answer A

50. What does this sign mean

A. Survey crew ahead

B. Filming crew ahead

C. Sightseeing ahead

D. Dancers ahead

Answer A

Chapter Five

Practice Test 4

1. What does this sign mean?

   A. Yield right of way
   B. Snow vehicle ahead
   C. Dead end ahead
   D. A Slow - moving vehicle ahead with the speed of 40km/h or less

Answer D

2. What does this sign mean?

   A. Lane ahead is closed for road work
   B. Bridge ahead
   C. The third lane bends to the left

D. Keep to the right of the traffic

Answer A

3. What does this sign mean:

A. Port route

B. Bridge ahead

C. Ferry service route

D. Ferry service Route

Answer D

4. What does this sign mean?

A. Detour route (temporary)

B. Construction work ahead

C. Road winding ahead

D. Closed lane ahead

Answer A

5. **If a school bus with flashing red light stop, you should:**
   A. Stop 20 meters away
   B. Reduce your speed and move with care
   C. Sound your horn as you approach
   D. Wait for oncoming vehicles to pass

Answer A

6. **A driver that is approaching a stop sign must:**
   A. Accelerate without stopping.
   B. Slow down then proceed if the way is clear
   C. Slow down then sound the horn and proceed
   D. None of the above

Answer B

7. **The minimum speed to give while following another vehicle is:**
   A. A two - second gap to the vehicle ahead
   B. 7 car lengths to the car ahead
   C. One second gap to the car ahead
   D. 5 car lengths to the car ahead

Answer A

8. **The key to the emergency braking**
   A. Steer to the left

B. Steer to the right
C. Try to lock the wheels
D. Stop the vehicle immediately without locking the wheels

Answer D

9. What should you do before moving off from a parked position?

A. Check for traffic, signal and pull away from the curb as fast as possible
B. Sound your horn and slowly pull away from the curb
C. Signal and pull away from the curb
D. Signal and check for traffic always, pulling out when it is safe to do so.

Answer D

10. What does this sign mean?

A. Indicates what services and facilities are located nearby or off - road
B. Indicates the services and facilities that are not available nearby or off-road

C. Shows only airport nearby

D. Shows the presence of police, an information desk, hospital and an airport in one building

Answer A

11. **Which of the vehicle has the right of way on a merging highway?**
    A. High speed moving vehicle
    B. Vehicles already on the highway
    C. Vehicle merging onto the highway
    D. None of the above

Answer D

12. **What action must you take if you intend to make a right turn on a red light?**
    A. Slow down
    B. Sound your horn and inform other drivers that you are coming
    C. Maintain a constant speed
    D. Come to a complete stop, give right of way to traffic and pedestrians before turning

Answer D

13. **How many times is it advised to check your rearview mirror when driving in urban areas?**
    A. Every 30 seconds

B. When slowing or stopping only

C. Every 8-12 seconds

D. Every 15-17 seconds

Answer C

14. **What weight should a child reached before he/she is switched from a rear - facing to a forward - facing car seat**

    A. 10kg
    B. 15kg
    C. 12kg
    D. 20kg

Answer A

15. **What is the minimum following distance recommended if you are driving a large vehicle?**

    A. Six vehicles
    B. Five seconds
    C. Four seconds
    D. Seven seconds

Answer C

16. **Refusal to provide your breath sample to a police officer attracts what consequences:**

    A. You will be arraigned under the criminal code of Canada

B. Immediate suspension of your license until the criminal charge is resolute
C. You will be compelled to ignition interlock program
D. All of the above

Answer D

17. **Unless posted otherwise, Restrictions in playground zones are imposed from 8:30 am until:**
A. One hour after sunset
B. One hour before sunset
C. 7:00pm
D. 8:00pm

Answer A

18. **What should you do when you are approaching an intersection with a solid yellow line?**
A. Make u - turn
B. Accelerate and cross the intersection
C. Do not enter the intersection
D. Back up

Answer C

19. **When planning to make a right turn, you should look over your shoulder**
A. To make sure you are on the right lane

B. To make sure there is no vehicle beside you (blind spot).
  C. To make sure another vehicle is not in your front
  D. To make sure another vehicle is not at your back

Answer B

20. **What should you do if glare makes it difficult for you to see in the daytime or at night**
   A. Slow down your vehicle
   B. Drive faster
   C. Do nothing
   D. Continue to drive at the same speed

Answer A

21. **What is the maximum distance required by the law the wheels of the parked vehicle are supposed to be from the curb?**
   A. 20 cm
   B. 30cm
   C. 40 cm
   D. 50cm

Answer D

22. **The term "spaces cushion" means?**
   A. The space around the entire vehicle
   B. The space between the driver and another vehicle

C. The space between the airbag and the driver

D. The space between the rear seat passengers and the driver

Answer A

23. A class 5 operator's license holder may not operate:

A. A motorcycle

B. A mopped

C. A two - axle class 2 or 4 type vehicle without passengers

D. A two - axle single

Answer A

24. What is the cause of hydroplaning?

A. Ice on the roadway

B. A flat tire

C. Overinflated tires

D. When the tires are riding on top of the water

Answer D

25. Any driver involved in a collision must

A. Remain at the scene

B. May leave the scene

C. If the driver is at fault, he/she must remain at the scene.

D. Must remain at the scene if there is an injury

Answer A

26. Always make sure there is an extra space between your vehicle and the motorcycle while following a motorcycle because:

A. It takes motorcycles long distance to stop
B. It takes motorcycles very short distance to stop
C. Motorcycles have a larger blind spot
D. Motorcycles lack efficient brakes

Answer B

27. When you see a pedestrian is preparing to cross the street, you should:

A. Reduce the speed and carefully drive straight.
B. Tell the pedestrian to stop and move with care
C. Sound your horn and proceed
D. You must come to a complete stop, allow the pedestrian to cross before entering the crosswalk

Answer D

28. What should you do if your vehicle is equipped with ABS, and you need to perform emergency braking?

A. Apply stable light pressure to the brake pedal
B. Apply stable firm pressure to the brake pedal

C. Switch between hard and light pressure on the brake pedal
D. Pump the brake pedal until you achieve a complete stop.

Answer B

29. **What do you check for before you enter your vehicle?**
A. Children
B. Pedestrians
C. Oncoming traffic
D. All of the above

Answer D

30. **What is the right procedure when you want to take the next exit on a highway?**
A. Signal; move into the exit lane and slow down
B. Slow down the vehicle, move into the exit lane, and signal
C. Signal, slow down the vehicle, move into the exit lane
D. Slow down the vehicle, signal, move into the exit lane

Answer A

31. **Braking skid occurs:**

A. Driving too slowly
B. Making a turn fast
C. Applying brake too hard
D. Accelerating too hard will cause the wheels to spin

Answer C

32. You should avoid following any emergency vehicle that has its siren or lights operating within what distance:

A. 150 m
B. 350m
C. 50m
D. 250m

Answer A

33. Winter traction is affected by the slippery condition, in what manner should a driver drive during winter:

A. The same with summer condition
B. Slower
C. Faster
D. All of the above

Answer B

34. The correct way to check if there are no vehicles or cyclists in your blind spot is:

A. To sound the horn
B. Make a shoulder check
C. Give the right signal
D. Check the rearview mirror

Answer B

35. **What type of flashing lights are snowplows equipped with to make them more visible:**
A. Green and blue
B. Blue and red
C. Red and amber
D. Yellow

Answer C

36. **What should you avoid when fueling a vehicle?**
A. Use of cellular phone
B. Leaving your engine running
C. Smoke
D. All of the above

Answer D

37. **What are the disadvantages of using under - inflated tires and low tire pressure?**
A. Faster wear in tires
B. It increases fuel consumption
C. It reduces stopping distance

D. None of the above

Answer A

38. For ideal safety, your head restraint should be positioned so that the middle of it is level with:

A. The middle of your neck

B. The top of your head

C. Your jawline

D. The top of the ears

Answer D

39. When a stopped school bus has its red lights flashing, and a stop arm is extended, what should you do:

A. Make a u - turn

B. Come to a complete stop

C. Proceed with caution

D. Accelerate fast with speed

Answer B

40. If you pass your exit on a highway, what should you do?

A. Make a u - turn

B. Continue to the next exit

C. Back up

D. None of the above

Answer B

41. **If found guilty of impaired driving that caused injuries or death to another person(s)**
    A. You will pay $25,000 fine
    B. Your license will be suspended for 5 years
    C. Your license will be suspended for life
    D. All of the above

    Answer B

42. **A driver responsibility is to ensure that passengers ----years of age wear their seat belts**
    A. 17
    B. Over 16
    C. Under 21
    D. Under 16

    Answer D

43. **What should you do before you drive?**
A. Buckle up
B. Mirror adjustment
C. Head restraint adjustment
D. All of the above

Answer D

44. **Unless posted otherwise, on a school day afternoon, a school zone is busy between**

A. 3:00pm to 4:30pm
B. 4:00pm to 4:30pm
C. 4:00pm to 5:00pm
D. 3:30pm to 4:00pm

Answer A

45. **What can you do to prevent brake overheating when traveling downhill in a vehicle with a standard transmission?**
A. Change to neutral
B. Change to a higher gear
C. Change to a lower gear
D. Pump your brake regularly

Answer C

46. **You are obligated to attach a red flag (day) or red light (night) to a load which extends beyond the rear of your vehicle by:**
A. 25 cm
B. 1.5cm
C. 1m
D. 0.5m

Answer B

47. **The maximum speed permitted in Alberta urban areas is:**

A. 50km/h
B. 40km/h
C. 30km/h
D. 60km/h

Answer A

48. Be careful of a large vehicle backing because:
A. Large vehicles have bigger blind spots
B. Large vehicle's brakes are not effective.
C. The large vehicle does not possess rear mirrors
D. The large vehicles does not possess side mirrors

Answer A

49. When do you slow down if you want to exit a highway?
A. Before the signal is activated
B. In the case traffic
C. After you enter the deceleration lane
D. Before reaching the deceleration lane

Answer C

50. Third - party insurance required by every driver should not be less than:
A. $50,000
B. $200,000
C. $10,000

D. $100,000

Answer B

Chapter Six

Practice Test 5

1. **What age is required to get a class 7 learner's driver's license?**
   A. At least 14 years
   B. At least 13 years
   C. At least 18 years
   D. At least 16 years

Answer A

2. **What is threshold braking?**
   A. Pushing brake to the edge of safety
   B. Press hard till the wheels stop
   C. Continuous pumping of brake
   D. Using all the braking force available without locking the wheel

Answer D

3. **Is a motor vehicle operator allowed to back a vehicle into an intersection or a crosswalk in an urban area?**
   A. Yes
   B. No
   C. In traffic only
   D. With the provision of proper signals

Answer B

4. **What is the distance transport Canada permits that you should position yourself if your vehicle is equipped with an airbag system?**
   A. 5cm from the steering wheel
   B. 15 cm from the steering wheel
   C. 35 cm from the steering wheel
   D. 25 cm from the steering wheel

Answer D

5. **You should be very careful when the asphalt appears:**
   A. Dull and black
   B. Shiny and black
   C. Dull and white
   D. Shiny and black

Answer D

6. **Where should you begin your turn when turning from one two way street onto another**
   A. The left hand - lane
   B. Left of the centerline
   C. The right hand - lane
   D. All of the above

Answer A

7. **To look out for wild animal on the road, you should be very careful:**
   A. Around midday
   B. Midnight
   C. At dawn
   D. At dawn and dusk

Answer D

8. **What is the recommended hand position on the steering wheel?**
   A. The 9 o'clock and 3 o'clock position
   B. The 7 o'clock and 50'clock position
   C. The 8 o'clock and 3 o'clock position
   D. The 9 o'clock and 2 o'clock position

Answer A

9. **Who is allowed to have access to the shoulder of a high way under normal circumstances?**
   A. Pedestrians and bicycles
   B. Motorcycles
   C. Vehicles towing a trailer
   D. Slow - moving vehicles

Answer A

10. **What action should you take in a situation when an oncoming driver at night has not dimmed its high beam headlights?**
    A. Sound your horn
    B. Switch on your high beam
    C. Look down a bit to the right edge of your lane until the vehicle passes
    D. None of the above

Answer C

11. **You must wear your helmet when riding a bicycle if you are under:**
    A. 18
    B. 19
    C. 21
    D. 20

Answer A

12. **The legal document all drivers supposed to possess during driving are**
    A. Drivers license, vehicle registration and proof of insurance
    B. Driver's license
    C. Driver's license and proof of insurance
    D. Driver's license and vehicle registration

Answer A

13. You are prohibited from sounding your horn or revving up your engine in residential areas between the hours:
    A. 6p.m-6a.m
    B. 2p.m – 7 am
    C. 10 pm – 7 am
    D. 12 pm- 6 am

Answer C

14. You are not allowed to exceed the speed limit posted when passing another vehicle
    A. True
    B. False

Answer A

15. Make sure that your vehicle can be seen from----------in both directions when parking on a roadway outside an urban area.
    A. 150m
    B. 60m
    C. 130m
    D. 200m

Answer B

16. When you want to park a vehicle with manual transmission on a hill, always leave the parking brake on and the transmission in:

A. Neutral

B. The third gear

C. The fifth gear

D. The first gear

Answer D

17. If you receive a text while driving, you should:

A. Check your phone immediately

B. Reduce your speed and check your phone

C. Ignore until you have stopped in a safe place

D. Check your phone when stopped at the intersection

Answer C

18. **Reversing must be done in what manner:**

A. Slowly and carefully

B. When the path is clear

C. Through the rear window while looking over your right shoulder

D. All of the above

Answer D

19. **You should turn off your engine if you are going to stop longer than:**

A. 5 seconds

B. 10 seconds

C. 7 seconds

D. 3 seconds

Answer B

20. **The following options are necessary before you can get a learner's license except:**

A. You must pass a road test

B. You must have a valid identification

C. You must not be below 14 years of age.

D. You must pass a knowledge test on the rules of the road and vision screening

Answer A

21. **Air brakes endorsement is called**

A. "K" endorsement

B. "Q" endorsement

C. "A" endorsement

D. "H" endorsement

Answer B

22. **What must the driver in the right - hand lane do when approaching the end of the passing lane?**

A. Speed up and merge

B. Stop for two seconds

C. Slow down and merge

D. Merge safely with the traffic in the left that is moving in the same direction

Answer D

23. All of the options below are correct when moving from one lane to the other except:

A. Checking for traffic by using side and rearview mirror

B. Turn on the correct signal and check your blind spot

C. Sounding your horn

D. Make sure a change of lane is allowed

Answer C

24. Use of the cruise control feature is not prohibited in one of the following options:

A. Under ideal highway driving conditions

B. On winding roads

C. On wet, snowy, slippery or icy surfaces

D. In urban traffic

Answer A

25. How long do visitors or tourists from other countries allowed to use valid operator's licenses:

A. 12 months

B. 6 months

C. 3 months

D. 9 months

Answer C

26. **What should you do when you enter the right - hand curve?**

A. Adjust your speed and shift to a lower gear

B. Drive slightly towards the right side of the road

C. Drive slightly towards the center of the road

D. Drive slightly towards the left side of the road

Answer B

27. **You must slow down to -------when you see a yellow flashing pedestrian - activated traffic light**

A. 60km/h

B. 40km/h

C. 30km/h

D. 50km/h

Answer C

28. **The vehicle to be used in road test must be in acceptable working conditions and must have:**

A. A spare tire

B. Signal lights

C. A heater

D. Rear Seats

Answer B

29. Long trucks require one of the following options:

A. More stopping time only
B. More turning space only
C. Wider lanes only
D. Additional time and space for starting, turning and stopping

Answer D

30. When you want to apply for a photo identification card, you must have all of the following except:

A. If you are under 18 years of age, you must get written consent from parent or guardian
B. Be an Alberta resident
C. Pass the road test
D. Provide acceptable identification

Answer C

31. Proactive driving can be described as:

A. Moving as fast as you can to reach your destination against all odd
B. Be observant and look out for potential hazards

C. Minimize your following distance

D. Text and receive a call while driving

Answer B

32. **A vehicle that pulls strongly to the right indicates:**

    A. Transmission failure

    B. Left side tire failure

    C. Brake failure

    D. Right side tire failure

Answer D

33. **What will be the result of fines incurred while speeding in work areas when workers are present?**

    A. Doubled

    B. Tripled

    C. Waived

    D. All of the above

Answer A

34. **What does this sign mean?**

A. Slippery pavement
B. Ice on the bridge
C. Chances of hydroplaning ahead
D. Winding road ahead

Answer A

35. What does this sign mean?

A. Narrow bridge ahead
B. Ice on the bridge
C. Broken bridge ahead
D. The Bridge ahead swings or lifts to let boats pass

Answer D

36. What does this sign mean?

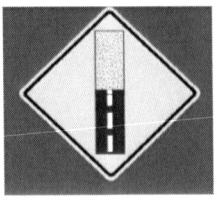

A. Paved road ending soon

B. Runway for airport ahead

C. Road ends soon

D. Two - way road ahead

Answer A

37. What does this sign mean?

A. Steep hill ahead, drive carefully

B. Truck garage ahead

C. Truck Entrance ahead

D. Construction zone ahead

Answer A

38. What does this sign mean?

A. Merging road ahead
B. Hidden intersection ahead
C. One way street ahead
D. None of the above

Answer A

39. What does this sign mean?

A. Flowing water on the road
B. Bridge ahead
C. Broken road pavement ahead
D. Icy bridge ahead

Answer A

40. Towing a trailer in Alberta is prohibited if one of the following options is on it:

A. Pets

B. Flammable materials

C. Persons

D. Firearms

Answer C

41. What must you do if a red X signal is displayed over your lane?

A. Stop immediately

B. Increase your speed

C. Be on an alert to stop

D. Do not go farther in this lane

Answer D

42. What should you do when merging on a freeway?

A. Drive slowly and be prepared to stop for freeway traffic

B. Halt on the acceleration lane, wait for a space in freeway traffic and enter fast

C. Signal, accelerate quickly to freeway speed and merge with flowing traffic

D. Slow down and then enter the traffic

Answer C

43. A white diamond marking shows that:

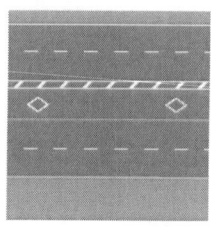

A. The lane will end soon
B. The lane is kept for certain vehicles
C. Railway crossing ahead
D. Only for commercial vehicle

Answer B

44. What is the consequence of driving with underinflated tires?

A. It reduces stopping distance
B. Faster tire wear
C. It improves fuel consumption
D. All of the above

Answer B

Manufactured by Amazon.ca
Acheson, AB